Seventh Day Baptist General Conference

An Appeal for the Restoration of the Bible Sabbath

In an Address to the Baptists

Seventh Day Baptist General Conference

An Appeal for the Restoration of the Bible Sabbath
In an Address to the Baptists

ISBN/EAN: 9783337170356

Printed in Europe, USA, Canada, Australia, Japan

Cover: Foto ©Lupo / pixelio.de

More available books at **www.hansebooks.com**

AN APPEAL

FOR THE

RESTORATION OF THE BIBLE SABBATH:

IN AN

ADDRESS TO THE BAPTISTS,

FROM

THE SEVENTH-DAY BAPTIST GENERAL CONFERENCE.

STEAM PRESS OF THE REVIEW AND HERALD OFFICE,
BATTLE CREEK, MICH.

1860.

THE ADDRESS.

The Seventh-day Baptist General Conference, to the Members of the Baptist Denomination throughout the United States, holding to the Observance of the First Day of the Week as a Divine Institution.

BELOVED BRETHREN: When our Divine Redeemer dwelt on earth, he prayed that all his disciples might be made perfect in one. As this prayer was in harmony with the sure word of prophecy, which instructs us to look for a time when "the watchmen shall see eye to eye, and sing with united voice," we are sure that it will ultimately be answered. We see nothing, however, to warrant us in looking for such a happy consummation, while we contemplate the multiplied divisions of the Christian world, perpetuated as they are by the selfishness of human nature. Here the prospect is dark indeed. But we have an unshaken confidence in the power of God to bring about his own purposes,* notwithstanding all the devices of men. "The hearts of all are in his hands, and he turneth them whithersoever he will." He that made "the multitude of one heart and of one soul," in the first age of the church, can again

---

* We do not look for the unity of the great religious bodies upon Bible truth ; but we do believe that God will "take out of them a people for his name," who will exhibit the unity expressed in Eph. iv; John xvii; Rom. xv, 6, 7; 1 Cor. i, 10; Col. iii, 1–4; 1 Pet. iii, 8.   PUBS.

concentrate his scattered bands, break down every wall of separation, and enlighten every mind by the effusion of his Spirit. Then shall Zion move forth, "clear as the sun, and terrible as an army with banners."

We rejoice, brethren, that you, as well as ourselves, are looking for this day of glory. Moreover, we have knowledge of your firm persuasion, that this glorious union of the now scattered forces of Israel, can be effected only upon the basis of divine truth. With a single glance you see the fallacy of that reasoning, which calls upon you, for the sake of union, to sacrifice the least particle of God's word. Taught by the Spirit of God, you have learned that the smallest atom of truth is more precious than fine gold. That meager piety which finds "non-essentials" in the appointments of Jehovah, you cannot abide. Your language is, "We esteem ALL thy precepts concerning ALL things to be right, and we hate EVERY false way."

We know, moreover, that it is the desire of your hearts, that all dissensions between Christians should be forever ended. For this object you are laboring and praying ; and while you are doing so, you have the enlightened conviction, that your labors and prayers will be successful, in proportion to the amount of truth with which your own minds are imbued, and which you can bring to bear upon the minds of others. Laboring as you are to expound to others the way of the Lord more perfectly, we cannot suppose that you are yourselves unwilling to learn. We therefore approach you with confidence, affectionately and earnestly requesting you to take into consideration the subject which is the only ground of difference between you and us. In our estimation, it is a subject of great importance; and though some of you have made it a matter of thought, we are persuaded that the great body of your denomination have dismissed it without any particular investigation. Indeed, we speak not unadvisedly when we say, that on this question the whole church of God have been hushed to sleep. In urging it upon your attention, we think you will not charge us with wishing to raise disturbance in Zion. We indulge the hope that you will impute to us the same disinterestedness of motive by which you yourselves are actuated when you boldly proclaim your denominational sentiments upon every high place, and scatter your publications in every direction. Your course springs not from any wish to foment disturbance, but from the pain which your hearts feel to see the institutions of Christ made void by the traditions of men. Our action in this matter springs from the same principle. We feel in regard to the Sabbath just as you do in regard to baptism. We declare before God and the Lord Jesus Christ, that we are moved by a desire for your good and God's glory.

When we look over your large and influential denomination, we find that, in reference to the subject upon which we now address you, you are divided into about three classes. 1. Those who, acknowledging the perpetuity of the Sabbath law, enforce the observance of the Sabbath by the fourth commandment, but change the day of its celebration from the seventh to the first day of the week. 2. Those who see the impossibility of proving a change of the day, and therefore regard the commandment as abolished by the death of Christ. But, at the same time, they consider the first day of the week as an institution entirely new, to be regulated as to its observance wholly by the New Testament. 3. Those who consider neither the Old nor the New Testament to impose any obligation upon them to observe a day of rest, and advocate one merely on the ground of expediency.

I.   To those of you who acknowledge the obligation of a Sabbath, but change the day of its celebration from the *seventh* to the *first* day of the week, we would say, that while from the law only you infer any obligation to sabbatize at all, yet make the particular time of sabbatizing to stand upon New Testament authority, we do not see how you can relieve yourselves from the charge of departing from the great principle contended for by Baptists; viz., That whatever is commanded by an institution, is to be learned from the law of the institution, and not from other sources.   On this principle, you reject the logic of Pedobaptists, who, while they find the ordinance of *baptism* in the New Testament, go back to the law of *circumcision* to determine the subjects.   You tell them, and very justly too, that the *law* of the institution is the *only rule* of obedience.   But do you not fall into the same error when the argument has respect to the Sabbath ?   We can see no more fitness in applying the law of the Sabbath to the first day of the week, than in applying the law of circumcision to the subjects of baptism.   For the law of circumcision was not more expressly confined to the fleshly seed of Abraham, than was the law of the Sabbath to the seventh day of the week. The true principle is, that every institution is to be explained and regulated by its own law. Therefore, if the first day of the week is an institution binding upon us, the law to regulate its observance should be looked for where we find the institution. Be pleased, brethren, to review this argument, and see if you are not treading on Pedobaptist ground.

In justification of this change of the day, we often hear you plead the example of Christ and his apostles. But where do we find anything to this effect in their example? Did the apostles *sabbatize* on the first day of the week? Did the churches which were organized by them do so? Observe, the question between you and us is NOT, Did they *meet together* and *hold worship* on that day? BUT, Did they *sabbatize?* that is, Did they REST FROM THEIR LABOR on the first day of the week? Did they observe it AS a Sabbath? This is the true issue. We have often asked this question, but the only answer that we have received has been, *that they assembled for worship.* But this is not a candid way of meeting the point. It is in reality an answer to a very different question from the one we ask. Brethren, act out your own principles. Come up fairly to the question. When you ask a Pedobaptist, Did Christ baptize or authorize the baptism of little children? you expect him to make some other reply than, "*He put his hands on them and prayed.*" When you ask, Did the apostles baptize unconscious babes? you are not well pleased with the reply, *They baptized*

households. Your question was with regard to
infants—the *baptism* of them.   If, therefore when
we ask you, Did the apostles and primitive Christians *sabbatize* on the first day of the week ? you
merely reply as above, we do not see but you are
guilty of the very same sophistry you are so ready
to charge upon your Pedobaptist brethren.   Your
adroit evasion of the real question seems to place
you much in the same predicament as were the
Pharisees, when Christ asked them whence was
the baptism of John.   It appears as if you rea-
soned with yourselves, and said, " If we shall say
they *did* sabbatize on the first day of the week,
the evidence will be called for, and we cannot find
it ; but if we shall say they did *not*, we fear the
day will lose its sacredness in the eyes of the people."   We do not by any means wish to charge
you with a Pharisaic lack of principle, but we
put it to your sober judgment, whether your position is not an awkward one.   Brethren, re-con-
sider this point, and see if you are not on Pedobaptist ground.

If the apostles did not sabbatize on the first day
of the week, then it follows, as a matter of course,
that whatever notoriety or dignity belonged to
that day, they did not regard it as a substitute for
the Sabbath.   Consequently, unless the Sabbath
law was entirely abrogated by the death of Christ,
the old Sabbath, as instituted in Paradise, and re-
hearsed from Sinai, continues yet binding, as "the
Sabbath of the Lord thy God."

But more than this.   Even if it could be proved,
that the apostles and primitive Christians *did* actually regard the first day of the week *as a Sab-*

bath, it would not follow that the old Sabbath is no longer in force, unless it could be proved that they considered the new as a SUBSTITUTE for the old; or, that so far as the particular day was concerned, it was of a CEREMONIAL character. But where do we find proof for either of these points? In the whole record of the transactions and teachings of the apostles, where do we find this idea of *substitution?* Nowhere. Where do we find evidence that, so far as the *particular day* was concerned, it was *ceremonial*, and therefore to cease at the death of Christ? Nowhere. The argument that proves the *Sabbath law* not to be ceremonial, proves the same of the *day*. Did the *Sabbath law* originate in Paradise, when man was innocent, and had no need of a Redeemer? So did the *day*. It was then sanctified and blessed. Does the *Sabbath law* take cognizance of the relation on which all the precepts of the moral law are founded; viz., the relation we sustain to God as *creatures* to *Creator?* So does the *day*. It is a memorial of this relation, and of the rest entered into by God after he, by his work, had established the relation. It appears, then, that neither the *Sabbath law*, nor the *day* it enjoins, was of a ceremonial character. True, it is not *moral*, in the strictest sense, but rather *positive*. Nevertheless, by divine appointment it is in the same category with the moral law, and must be considered a part of it. If this reasoning is correct—and if it is not, we hope you will point it out—it would not follow that the old Sabbath is done away, because Christ and his apostles sab-

2

batized on the first day of the week ; but only
that there were *two* Sabbaths instead of *one*.

But could Christ or his apostles consistently al-
ter the law of the Sabbath ?   In all his ministry,
Christ acted under the *appointment* of the Father,
and according to such *restrictions* as were contained in the law and the prophets.   By those restrictions, no laws were to be set aside at his com-
ing, except such as were peculiar to the Jewish
economy ; such as " meats, and drinks, and divers
washings, and carnal ordinances, imposed until
the time of reformation."   Heb. ix, 10.   To set
aside these, the law gave the Messiah an express
grant.   Heb. x, 9.   But the very moment he
should attempt to go beyond the limits of that
grant, he would destroy all evidence of his being
the Messiah promised and appointed.   For it was
by his exact conformity to the law, that his claims
were established.   Hence, early in his ministry,
he declared that he " came not to *destroy* the law
or the prophets."   Matt. v, 17.   Most cheerfully
do we recognize him as God over all, and blessed
forever ; yet we are well satisfied that, even in
virtue of his divinity, he could not consistently set
aside any laws except those which were " a shad-
ow of things to come."   Otherwise we should
have God *denying* himself—God *contradicting*
himself !   The New Testament records not a single instance of his claiming a right to do so.   When
he avowed himself Lord of the Sabbath, he only
claimed to determine what was the proper method
of keeping it—what were breaches of it, and what
were not.   The Sabbath was made *for* man, and

consequently it was his prerogative to decide what acts and duties answered to the nature and design of the institution. *Therefore*, the Son of man is Lord of the Sabbath. Mark ii, 28.

In regard to the obligation resulting from apostolic example, it appears to us that you have fallen into some errors. We are not convinced that the example of the apostles can be justly pleaded for anything else than the order and arrangement of the *church*. However proper it may be to imitate them in other respects—in the duties of the moral law, for instance—yet, if it were not known to be proper, independent of their example, we cannot suppose their example would make it so. We must first ascertain, by some settled and infallible rule, whether their practice is worthy of imitation. In regard to the ordering of *church affairs*, there can be no doubt, for they were sent upon this very errand, with the promise of the Holy Spirit to qualify them for the work. But the Sabbath is not a *church ordinance*. It is not an institution for the church *as such*, but for *all mankind*. All reasoning with reference to it, from apostolic example, must therefore be very inconclusive. Even if we should admit that the *church* is bound by such example to regard the first day of the week, yet this is the utmost extent to which our admissions can go. We cannot see how the institution becomes binding upon the world at large. Consequently, we are compelled to maintain, that an institution which was originally given for all mankind, remains unaltered. We are willing that the example and practice of the apostles should regulate the *church* as to its ordinances and

government, and herein we claim to follow them
as strictly as you do ; but when they are pleaded
for anything more, we want first to know whether
they conform to the express law of God.   Otherwise we must consider them as no more binding
than an apostle's quarrel with Barnabas.   Acts
xv, 39.

If this argument is well founded, we are led to a
very satisfactory disposal of a question often pro-
posed ; viz., Why do we never read in the New
Testament of Christian assemblies being convened
as such on the Sabbath ?   For if the Sabbath be
not a *church ordinance*, but an institution for mankind at large, it can be of no importance for us to
know what Christian assemblies *as such* did with
regard to it.   All that is of real importance for
us to know, is the precise bearing of the institution upon man *as* man—upon man *as* a rational
and accountable creature.   On this point the in-
formation is clear and decisive.

The controversy between us and you appears to
be brought down to a very narrow compass.   *Did
the apostles and primitive Christians sabbatize on
the first day of the week ?*   And, *Is it the duty of
all men to imitate their example, or only the* CHURCH ?
If, upon a solemn and prayerful consideration of
this subject, you are persuaded that there is no
proof that the early Christians regarded the first
day as a Sabbath (substituted in place of the seventh), and will honestly avow your conviction, we
have no fear that the controversy will be prolong-
ed.   For, should you still be of opinion that some
sort of notoriety was attached to the day, and that
Christians met for worship, we shall not be very

ADDRESS TO THE BAPTISTS.   13

solicitous to dispute the point.   The apostolic rule, " Let every man be fully persuaded in his own mind," will then govern us.   See Rom. xiv, 5, 6. Our concern is not that you keep the first day of the week, but that you keep it *in place of the Sabbath*, thus making void the commandment of God. If once you discover that Sunday is not the Sabbath by divine appointment, and therefore cannot be enforced upon the conscience, we are persuaded that your deep sense of the necessity of such an institution, will soon bring you to the observance of the one originally appointed.

II.   But we proceed to address those of you who regard the sabbatic law as having been nailed to the cross, and consider the first day of the week as an institution entirely new, regulated as to its observance wholly by the New Testament.

You, whom we now address, are exempt from some of the inconsistencies which we have exposed ; but your theory labors under very serious difficulties, and is to be regarded, on the whole, as more obnoxious to the interests of religion, than the one we have been considering.

According to your position, the New Testament recognizes no Sabbath at all.   Do not start at this charge.   That it is repugnant to your feelings, we allow.   You have never thought of anything else than *entire abstinence from labor* on the first day of the week.   It is your day of *rest*, as well as *worship*.   But on what ground do you make it a day of rest ?   What *example* have you for doing so ?   What *law* of the New Testament requires you to lay aside all your secular business ? As sin is the transgression of the law, and where

no law is there is no transgression [1 John iii, iv ;
Rom. iv, 15], how do you make it appear to be
sin to work on the day in question? It is by the
commandment that sin becomes exceeding sinful.
Rom. vii, 13. By what commandment do you
make it appear sinful to work on Sunday? These
are questions of the highest importance.

Now suppose one of your brethren attends public worship on the first day of the week, and—to
make his conformity to what is supposed to be
apostolic example as perfect as possible—participates in the breaking of bread. He then goes
home, and labors diligently till the day is closed.
By what law will you convince him of sin? Not
the law of the Sabbath as contained in the Decalogue, for that you hold to be abolished. Not any
law of the New Testament which says, " Keep the
first day of the week holy ; in it thou shalt not do
any work," for there is no such law. Not the law
of apostolic example, for there is no proof that
the apostles ever gave such example. The very
utmost that you can with any show of reason pretend of their example is, that they met together
for worship and breaking of bread. To this example your brother has conformed to the very letter—who can say he has not in spirit also? What
now will you do with him? " The Bible, and the
Bible only, is the religion of Protestants." The
Bible, therefore, is the rule by which he is to be
tried. Convict him of sin by this rule, if you can.

But the case becomes still more difficult, when
you come to apply it to those who are without the
pale of the church. We have already seen that
apostolic example concerns merely the ordering

and arrangement of the *church*. Attempt now to convince the unbeliever of sin in working on the first day of the week. In order to do this, charge apostolic example upon him. What is his reply? "I know not," says he, "that I am bound to imitate them in this matter. How does it appear that I am? I will admit, for argument's sake, that they celebrated the resurrection on Sunday by religious worship; but they also broke bread and partook of it by way of celebrating his death. If their example binds me in one particular, why not in the other? Prove to me," says he, "that any but the church assembled on the first day for worship, and I will do so too. But in the absence of all such proof, I must conclude that their example has nothing to do with me; unless, indeed, you can make it appear that their example and practice were in conformity to some law, which commanded them as rational creatures, independent of their relation to Christ and his church. When you can produce that law, then I shall feel bound to obey it, and imitate the apostles in their obedience to it; but not till then." Such is the reasoning by which an unbeliever may set aside all your attempts to charge sin upon him. Where, brethren, is your law which, like a barbed arrow, pierces the very soul, and fastens guilt upon the conscience? Where is that law which speaks out its thunders, saying, "Thus saith the Almighty God, the Lord, the maker of heaven and earth, It is the Sabbath-day; in it thou shalt not do any work?" To throw aside the law, which cuts and flames every way, reaching soul and spirit, joints and marrow, in order to deal with the ungodly by

mere apostolic example, is like muffling the sword,
lest it should give a deadly wound.   Apostolic example is indeed powerful with those whose hearts
have been made tender by the Spirit of God, but
with others powerless.

We are persuaded, brethren, that your consci-
entious scruples about laboring on the first day of
the week, never resulted from the mere contemplation of apostolic example.   Such example, it
is true, is all the law you acknowledge ; but this
is the theory you have adopted since you came to
maturity, and began to think for yourselves.   Your
scruples have an earlier and different origin.   They
commenced with your childhood, when you were
taught to consider the day as holy time.   It was
then carefully instilled into your mind, that God
had, by express law, forbidden you to desecrate
the day, and that you would incur his displeasure
in case you should do so.   The idea was then im-
bibed, that if you did not keep the day, you would
violate the fourth commandment.   This idea has
grown with your growth, and strengthened with
your strength.   It has obtained such commanding
influence over your feelings, that you cannot com-
fortably forbear keeping a day of rest, though
your theory does not require it.   Even to this day
a strong impression rests upon your minds, that
the fourth commandment contains much of moral
excellence—too much to be thrown altogether
away, notwithstanding your system of theology
teaches its abrogation.   Such is the true secret of
your tenderness of conscience.   Apostolic example has in reality nothing to do with it.   Following the secret monitions of conscience, your pros-

perity is promoted in spite of your theological system. But sound reason discovers that your experience and your theory are in opposition to each
other. Some of the more thinking ones among
you are aware of this, and are continually aiming
at such a modification of their theory, that their
experience will harmonize with it. But be as-
sured, that there will be an everlasting conflict,
till you are brought to acknowledge fully and
heartily the claims of the sabbatic law.

We are aware of that system of theology which
regards the New Testament as furnishing the only
code of laws by which men are bound since the
death of Christ. We have looked at this doctrine
with attention; and so far as the order, government, and ordinances of the *church* are concerned,
we admit its truth. As the laws and ordinances
of the *Jewish* church were determined by the *Old*
Testament, so the laws and ordinances of the
Christian church are determined solely by the *New*
Testament. Therefore, we should say at once,
the argument is yours, if the Sabbath were a
church ordinance. In such case, however, none
but the church has a Sabbath. But the question
is not concerning church ordinances. In these we
follow the New Testament as closely as yourselves
The question is concerning an institution which
has respect to mankind at large—to man *as* man;
for the Saviour teaches us that the Sabbath was
made *for* man. Now, it will be a very hard matter to prove that when men as rational creatures
are concerned, the only code of laws by which
they are bound is the New Testament. Let us
put the matter to the test. How will you prove

that it is unlawful for a man to marry his sister, his daughter, or any other of near kin ? The New Testament utters not a word on the subject. It is not enough to say, It is implied in the law which forbids adultery ; for it must first be proved to be a species of adultery to do so. Nor will it do to say, The common sense of mankind is a sufficient law on the subject ; for the moment we suppose that its unlawfulness is to be determined in this way, we abandon the argument that the New Testament is the only code of laws, and resort to the common sense of mankind as furnishing a part of the code. But if the common sense of mankind shall furnish a part of the code by which we are bound, who shall undertake to say how large a part ? Besides, on this principle, the book of divine revelation is not complete and perfect. It is a lamp to our feet only in part, and the common sense of mankind makes out the deficiency ! You are, therefore, driven to take your stand again upon the New Testament. Finding you there again, we repeat the question, *How do you prove by your code that a man may not marry his sister ?* It is impossible. You must, of necessity, look to that division of the Scriptures usually called the Old Testament ; for the New says not one word about it.

Let us turn now to the 18th chapter of the book of Leviticus, and we shall find a collection of laws exactly to the point. " None of you shall approach to any that is near of kin to him," &c. Verse 6. The degrees of kindred are then expressly marked. Will it be objected, that these laws were given particularly to the Jews, and to no other people? We admit they were given to the Jews, as indeed was the whole system of revelation in that age; but we cannot admit that they concerned no other class of people. For it is expressly shown in that chapter, that the matters of which they took cognizance, were regarded as abominations in the Gentiles. Because of such things, the fierce wrath of Jehovah came down upon the Canaanites, and they were cast out of the land as loathsomeness. Verses 24, 30. If these things were viewed as abominable in the Canaanites, they surely were not *ceremonial* pollutions. They were not mere *Jewish* laws. The fallacy of the doctrine is therefore sufficiently exposed.

We think you have fallen into error concerning the nature and design of that division of the Scriptures commonly called the New Testament. We regard it not as the *Law Book* of mankind, in the strict and proper sense; but rather as a *Treatise on Justification*, or an *Expose of the Way of Salvation*, in which are contained such references to the law, and such quotations from it, as are necessary to the complete elucidation of the subject. The preparation of this treatise was of necessity delayed until the great Sacrifice for sin had been offered, and our High Priest had entered into the holy place. For, as the sacrifice and intercession of our High Priest constitute the sole foundation of our justification, so " the way into the holiest of all was not yet made manifest, while the first tabernacle was yet standing." Heb. ix, 8. So much of the plan of salvation was illustrated to the people, as could be by means of the ritual service; and that, together with the prophecies, laid a foundation for them to *believe* that, *in some way or other*, they would be just before God. So that by *faith* the patriarchs were justified. Heb. xi. They knew it was to be *somehow* through the work of him who was typified and promised as the great Redeemer. But they could not understand the plan until the Redemer came and died for them.

Because this expose of the way of salvation could not be made until after the death of the High Priest, *therefore* it was not proper to organize gospel churches. The only church that was suitable for that age was found in the Jewish nation, and from its very nature was unfit for the world at large. It was, therefore, confined to that people. Moreover, because it was not proper to organize gospel churches until the way of salvation was fully laid open, it was also not proper to lay down the laws and ordinances of the church until that time. This accounts for the laws of the church being found only in the New Testament.

Now, if the New Testament is to be regarded as an exhibition of the way of salvation, with such references to the Old as are necessary for the elucidation of the subject, rather than as the Law Book for mankind at large, the idea that the Sabbath ought not to be looked for in the Old Testament, falls to the ground. Nevertheless, to some minds it appears strange that while the New Testament writers mention all the other duties of the Decalogue, this of Sabbath-keeping is apparently omitted. In speaking of the sins of which Christians were guilty before their conversion, not one word is said about Sabbath-breaking, though upon other sins they dwell with emphasis. But this

admits of a very easy solution.   Those writers addressed two classes of converts—those from among
the Jews, and those from among the Gentiles.
As to the former, they were already rigid to an
extreme in keeping the Sabbath.   All that was
necessary to do in their case, was to vindicate the
institution from Pharisaic austerities, and determine what was lawful to be done, and what was
not lawful.   This was done by Christ.   But as for
the Gentile converts, to charge them with having
been guilty of the sin of Sabbath-breaking in their
state of heathenism, would have been manifest im-
propriety.   For the Sabbath being for the most part
a *positive* rather than a *moral* precept, it could not
be known without a revelation.   But as the Gentiles had no revelation, this is a good reason why
the apostle dwelt not upon this sin, to charge it
upon them, but those only which were more obvi-
ously breaches of the Moral Law.   Thus it appears, there was no necessity for any more particular mention of the Sabbath to be made in the New
Testament than what is made.

But it is not our object in this Address to cover
the whole field of argument.   We design simply,
by presenting some of the strong points, and exposing your inconsistencies, to stir up your attention to the subject.   We are sure that the great
majority of you have never given it a thorough
investigation.   For a complete discussion of the
whole ground we refer you to our publications.
Will you read them?   Will you anxiously inquire,
What is truth?   Will you pray over the matter,
saying, " Lord, what wilt thou have us to do?"

Or will you sleep over it as if it were of no great practical importance ?

III. But we must address that class of Baptists who consider neither the Old nor the New Testament to impose any obligation to observe a day of rest, and advocate one merely on the ground of expediency. In some sections of our country, Baptists would consider it almost a slander upon their denomination to intimate that there were persons among them of such anti-Sabbath principles. But any one who is conversant with the order at large, knows very well that it is true. There are those who boldly avow such doctrine, and many others who do not deny that it is their real sentiment, though they are not forward to proclaim it upon the house-tops. Whether this class embraces a very large proportion of the denomination, it is not necessary to inquire. It is our impression that the proportion is sufficiently large to justify an effort for their conversion to right views of Divine Truth.

If there is no day of rest enjoined by divine authority, and the observance of one rests wholly upon expediency, we see no reason, except that the voice of the multitude is against it, why you cannot as well observe the *seventh* as the *first* day of the week. There would be no sacrifice of conscience in so doing, while it would be a tribute of respect to those who feel that the keeping of the seventh day is an indispensable part of duty. But it is not on this principle, particularly, that we desire you to change your ground. Feeling that it is not *our party* that must be honored, but rather *divine truth,* and our party only *for the sake of* the truth, we would much rather correct your doctrinal views.

Of course you do not deny that a day of rest was once enjoined upon God's chosen people. It is only under the gospel that you suppose all distinction of days to be annihilated. If, then, it is *expedient* that a day of rest should be observed, it follows irresistibly, that the annihilation of all distinction in days, by the gospel, was very EXPEDIENT! And thus, whatever blessings the gospel dispensation brings to the human race, a strict following out of its principles would be INEXPEDIENT! And, farther, that the *law* which enjoined a day of rest, had more of an eye to expediency than the *gospel* has! Consequently that the gospel, though declared to be *faultless,* and capable of *perfecting* those who believe, must nevertheless, FOR EXPEDIENCY'S SAKE, borrow a little help from the abrogated rites of the law! In other words, God, in setting aside a day of rest, committed an oversight, and left his work for man to mend! Brethren, we see not how it is possible for you to escape such monstrous conclusions. They are the legitimate result of your principles—principles that you must have adopted without considering where they would land you. For we are not disposed to believe you so completely destitute of piety, as willingly to abide by the result of them. We entreat you to reconsider them, and adopt such as are more in accordance with the spirit of our holy religion.

When you advocate the observance of a day of rest on the ground of *expediency,* we are persuaded

that you do so in view of the bearing you perceive
it to have upon the well being of mankind. But
still the question will arise, Has the gospel less regard to the well being of mankind than the law
had ?   Look at the humanity of the Sabbatic institution.   How   necessary   that   both   man   and
beast should rest one day in seven.   How evident
that they cannot endure uninterrupted toil.   How
perfectly well established, that, if doomed to con-
stant labor, they sink under the premature exhaus-
tion of their powers. So well is this established that
we cannot put such a low estimate upon your judgment as to suppose it necessary to enter upon any
proof of it. But the question returns, Does the gospel breathe less humanity than the law ?   Or, consider the bearing of the institution upon the interests of religion.   It affords opportunity for men to
be instructed in the great things which pertain to
their salvation ; and if there were no Sabbath to
call them away from their labors, it would be impossible to bring religious instruction into contact
with their minds.   Does the gospel afford less advantage in this respect than the law did ?   Did
the law provide a season for instructing the people in religion as it *then* stood ? and does the gospel provide no season for instructing them in religion as it now stands ?   Must they be instructed
in *types*, but not in the *substance ?*—in *prophecy*,
but not in the *fulfillment* of prophecy ? No one
will be responsible for the affirmative of these
questions.

If the New Dispensation actually has abrogated
the Sabbath, we do not believe that it is *expedient*
to observe it.   We cannot believe, however, that an

institution so important to the civilization, refinement and religious prosperity of mankind, has been abrogated. We refer you to our publications, and to the publications of those who have, in common with us, defended the perpetuity of the Sabbatic law; and we entreat you to reconsider your ground. The doctrine of expediency! What a fruitful source of corruption has it been to the church of God! There is not an anti-Christian, popish abomination, but what pleads something of this kind. Do, dear brethren, let it be expunged from your creed.

BRETHREN OF THE BAPTIST DENOMINATION :— You are a great and growing people. Your influence is felt throughout the length and breadth of our land. We rejoice in your prosperity. "May the Lord make you to increase and abound in love one towards another, and toward all men." In your prosperity we behold, in a measure, our own. Your baptism is our baptism. Your church government is our government. Your doctrinal principles are ours; and there is nothing which constitutes any real ground of separation, except the great and important subject we now urge upon your attention.

The popularity you have gained as a denomination, however, is not owing to your Sabbath principles. It is founded entirely on your views concerning the initiating ordinance of the gospel. These views are characterized by that perfect simplicity which marks every divine institution. Hence you have won the affections of the common people, while, if you had attempted to operate on

them by a more complicatied theory, failure would
have been the result.

This induces us to urge upon your notice the
exceeding simplicity of the Sabbatarian argument,
compared with all those theories which stand in
opposition to it.   It is adapted to persons of weak
capacities.   Any illiterate person can open the
Bible, and point to the chapter and verse, saying,
" The seventh day is the Sabbath of the Lord thy
God."   This is plain ; he can understand it.   But
tell him that redemption was a much greater work
than creation; that redemption was finished by the
resurrection of Christ ; that an event so important
ought to be commemorated ; and that, in order to
do this, the day of the Sabbath was changed from
the seventh to the first day of the week ; for all
which there is not a single " thus saith the Lord,"
nothing but the uncertain deductions of human reason ; can he understand it?   No.   It requires an elevation of intellect which God has not
given him.   The inferences and deductions are beyond his capacities.   How then is he to render an *intelligent* obedience?   If he conform his
practice to the theory thus set before him, it will
not be because he understands it, but because he
is willing to trust the guidance of his mind to
those who, he thinks, know more than he does
himself.   This, therefore, is strong internal evidence that the keeping of the first day is not of
God.   For the book of God is adapted not only
to those of elevated intellect, but to the ignorant
and rude.   Everything concerning our practice is
plain even to wayfaring men.   Were it otherwise,

we should conclude that the Bible is not an inspired production.   If it did not come down to the capacities of all, we should infer that it was not made
by Him who made all minds.   Indeed, it would
not, in such case, be a *revelation* to all, but only
to the more talented.   But it is a revelation to *all;*
and he that obeys God must do it for himself; he
that repents and believes, must do so for himself;
and at the great day, every one of us shall give
account for himself unto God.   It is of the highest
importance, therefore, that every one knows *for
himself* the foundation of his faith and practice.

In thus urging the simplicity of the argument
for the Sabbath, we are but doing what you do in
regard to Baptism.   Compare the cases.   A man
of considerable intellect can reason from the Abrahamic covenant, lay propositions together, and
draw inferences and deductions, until, finally, he
makes it pretty clear to his own mind, that the
children of the flesh, these are the children of
God; Paul to the contrary notwithstanding.   But
how is it with some good old Baptist sister, who
can hardly join two ideas together, and draw a
logical inference from them?   Why, she cannot
tell about this reasoning from the Abrahamic covenant.   It is something she does not understand.
But she can open her Bible, and point to chapter
and verse for believers' baptism.   She puts her
finger upon something that is just adapted to her
capacities.   As she has a soul to save, an obedience to render, and an account to give, all for her-
self, her practice is accordingly.   Brethren, think
this matter over, and see whether your reasoning
on the Sabbath is not very much akin to that of

those who reason from the Abrahamic covenant to
Baptism. Think seriously, whether it does not
render *intelligent* obedience impossible to vast
numbers of Christians. Think whether a course
of reasoning which darkens a very simple subject,
is not more specious than solid.

Again, your children are to be early instructed
in this matter. How do you succeed in making
them understand it? Is your little child capable
of comprehending all this argument, which you
found upon the finishing of redemption by the resurrection of Christ? Can you point him to any
plain passage, where Christ authorizes a change
of the Sabbath? How do you feel when the little creature says, in the simplicity of his heart,
"Father, mother, does not the fourth commandment require the observance of the seventh day
of the week? But do we not keep the first day?
I should think this is not keeping the commandment." One would think you would be forcibly
reminded of that Scripture, "Out of the mouths
of babes and sucklings thou hast ordained
strength." Ps. viii, 2.

The extensive operations in which you are en-
gaged for the conversion of the world, render it
in the highest degree important that you should
not err on a question like this. If you are right,
you ought to be very certain of it. Among the
heathen, you are extending the observance of
Sunday as a sacred day. If you are thus sowing
the seeds of error instead of truth, the evils who
can calculate? Hence you cannot too early be-
gin to review your ground. Consider the difficulties your missionaries already have to encounter,

because of unscriptural sentiments propagated among the heathen by those who nevertheless loved their souls. The poor, perishing idolaters are witnesses of the clashing of doctrine between Jesus Christ's men, and they ask, " *Why is this? You have come to give us a gospel which professes to make its followers 'perfect in one,' and yet you yourselves are divided.*" You cannot in conscience abandon your principles, however, nor dare you, in your translations, give to a sentence or a particle one single turn, which will not fully express the mind of the Holy Spirit. Dare you, then, without feeling the most entire certainty, teach them that God says, " Remember the first day of the week to keep it holy ?" The responsibility of the missionary, in this respect, is not less than where his translation is concerned. Does he feel the same awful sense of responsibility ?

From the heathen turn to the contemplation of the Jewish nation.* The time cannot be far distant, when those who, " as touching the election, are beloved for the fathers' sakes," shall be called to behold the glory of God, in the face of Him they have so long rejected. But in order to this, a voice from the divine word cries, " Cast ye up, cast ye up, prepare the way, take up the stumbling block out of the way of my people." Have Christians seriously considered what this stumbling block is ? For our own part, we are persuaded that nothing can be more justly called by this

* The desecration of the Sabbath by professed believers in Christ, doubtless has been, and still is, a stumbling-block in the way of the Jews to keep them from Christ; but we see no promises for the " Jewish nation" more than for other unbelieving nations.—PUBS.

name, than the general abandonment, on the part of Christians, of the Sabbath of the Lord. The Jews, taking it for granted, without examination, that this abandonment is really taught by the Christian religion, suppose that its author cannot be the true Messiah. They have seen, through every period of their nation's history, that God has put signal honor upon this institution. They have seen its sacredness elevated high above that of the ceremonial institutions. They have heard their prophets dwell upon the profanation of it as the crying sin of the land, on account of which the sore judgments of Heaven came down upon it. It is true, some teach that the whole Mosaic system was clothed with as much sacredness as the Sabbath; and that it was not for the sin of Sabbath breaking, any more than for a disregard of the ritual service in general, that they suffered the wrath of Jehovah. But such persons must have paid only a superficial attention to the subject. The attentive reader cannot fail to be struck with the fact, that while in the prophets the Sabbath is exalted as of vast importance to the nation, and all its prosperity, and the favor of God, seemingly, suspended on the proper keeping of it, ceremonial usages are comparatively depreciated.

Since the Sabbath holds such a sacredness throughout the ancient oracles of God—since the Israelites have taken their lessons of obedience to it under "the rod of his wrath"—since no grant was given to the Messiah to set it aside, nor the least intimation ever made to the Jews that it would be set aside—can we wonder that they think that teacher to be an impostor who should break this commandment, and teach men so?

But there is a crisis approaching—the day is near, and it hasteth greatly—when it will be indispensable that all those who truly love the Lord Jesus Christ, have their "loins girt about with truth." Popery is preparing for another desperate struggle. The great principle of the Reformation, that "the Scriptures are the only rule of faith," is to be discussed anew. In the Church of England, this discussion has already commenced. Rome has opened her sluices, and anti-christian corruption again threatens to flood the church of God. As the water naturally seeks such channels as may already be prepared, so will it be with this doctrine. What branch of Zion will be next troubled? Probably that which makes the next widest departure from the great Protestant principle. Then that which is next in order; and so on. For it can not reasonably be expected to stop, until it reach that order of people which is governed by the Bible alone. Upon all others the desolation must be more or less extensive. For those who acknowledge the principle of departing from the Bible in ever so small a degree, may be expected to exemplify it to an indefinite extent, when the circumstances of the times are so modified as to give occasion for it. As for yourselves, you do not avow the *principle* of departing from the Scriptures, but profess to hold it in abhorrence. The language of your *creeds* is explicit on this point; and we know of no denomination so forward to plead a strict conformity to this principle as yourselves. Yet it is impossible for you to pre-

tend, with any show of modesty, that the Scriptures expressly enjoin the keeping of Sunday as a
Sabbath to the Lord. You cannot say, from
Scripture authority, that the apostles observed it
as such. Nevertheless, your creed declares that
it ought to be so observed; and your practice ac-
cords with your creed. Wherefore, it is as evident as mathematical demonstration, that you do
depart from the great Protestant principle. Consequently, if our views be correct in regard to the
crisis which is at hand, the time cannot be far distant, when your own denomination will in some
modified form be affected with the deprecated evil,
and you will be compelled to abandon every principle and practice which can give it the smallest
advantage.

Do you think, brethren, that in your present
position you are prepared for the great struggle?
When the Puseyite, replying to those who contend
for the Protestant maxim, refers to the observance
of Sunday, and says, "Here we are absolutely
compelled to resort to the aid of ancient usage,
as recorded, not by the inspired, but by the unin-
spired writers," are you ready for the issue? Can
you confute what he says? When another one
says, "The *seventh* day is the Sabbath of the
Lord thy God; we celebrate the *first*. Was this
done by divine command? No. I do not recol-
lect that the Saviour, or the apostles, say we shall
rest on the first day of the week instead of the
seventh;" and then concludes, "The same rea-
sons which urge you to dissent from the observance of the three grand festivals of the Church of
England, ought to operate with you respecting the

Sabbath ;"—are you prepared to join issue with him ? Can you justify yourselves on your own principles? If you can, we will confess our short-sightedness. But indeed we fear, we tremble, in view of the crisis which is approaching, when we look at the traditional usages prevailing among Christians, and consider with what a tenacious grasp they are held. O Lord God Almighty! thou who hast sworn that " thy kindness shall not depart from thy church, nor the covenant of thy peace be removed," let not thy truth fall in the contest.

We mean not to goad your feelings, by charging upon you any of the abominations of Popery. We are sure you would not cherish one of them, if you were conscious of it. But we take it for granted, that those who are forward to take the mote out of their brother's eye, are willing to have the beam taken out of their own. You have charged Pedobaptist denominations, over and over, with upholding Popery's chief pillar. You have told them, that their zeal, against the man of sin would avail them but little, until they first rid themselves of his traditions. You have talked feelingly of the sin of encumbering the ordinances of God with human inventions. You have read the church of Christ many a good lesson on the importance of holding the truth in its purity. In all this you have, doubtless, been sincere. We have no fault to find with you ; for you have only followed the Bible direction, " Cry aloud, spare not, show my people their transgression." In conformity with this direction, we would endeavor to act our part as faithful reprovers. Yet our de-

sire is, to do it with meekness, considering ourselves lest we also be tempted. It may be—we
know not—that some of the abominations of the
man of sin are cleaving to us. If so, "let the
righteous smite us, it shall be a kindness; let
them reprove us, it shall be an excellent oil, which
shall not break our head."

Turn, brethren, to the seventh chapter of the
prophecy of Daniel, and twenty-fifth verse. You
there find one spoken of who "shall speak great
words against the Most High, and shall wear out
the saints of the Most High, *and think to change*
TIMES *and* LAWS." You have had no difficulty in
finding in this prophecy a reference to the law of
baptism, as one of the *laws* which this great power has changed; but you have not shown satisfac-
torily what are the *times*. You have usually referred them to the numerous festivals and holy-
days, which have been multiplied by the church of
Rome. But these were *times* ESTABLISHED; not
times CHANGED. Will you please to expound this
passage a little more clearly? Will you tell us
whether, under the gospel, there is any sacred
time except the Sabbath? We will not be unrea-
sonably confident, but we are much mistaken, if
you can give any clear and satisfactory construc-
tion to this prophecy, without finding that something of Rome still cleaves to you.

Suffer us here to declare our conviction, that
you could take no more effectual step toward con-
verting the Christian world to right views about
baptism, than to embrace the Sabbath of the Bible. In your discussions with Pedobaptists, you
are constantly referred to the change of the Sab-

bath, as proof that some things may be binding which the Scriptures do not expressly enjoin. You have never met this argument fairly and fully. To be sure, you always make an attempt to meet it. But how do you do it? By proving that Christ expressly enjoined his followers to *sabbatize* on the first day of the week? By showing from express scripture testimony, that the apostles *did actually rest from their labors* on that day? No. Neither of these things have you ever shown; nor can you show them. The whole head and front of your proof—if proof it may be called— amount only to this : that the apostles and primitive Christians *met together for worship* on that day. It is true, by such a course you have generally talked your opponents into silence, because by exposing fully the defect of your reply, it would only render their own transgression the more glaring. But while you *silenced* them, you did not *convince* them. While they saw that for one of *your own* customs you could not plead a "thus saith the Lord," they felt comparatively easy under all your rebukes, and naturally enough thought it not *very* important, that *they* should should have a "thus saith the Lord" for the sprinkling of babes.

But a most important consideration, in view of this subject, is the influence of your large and powerful denomination upon an unconverted world. Whatever your theory about the perpetuity of the sabbatic law—whatever your doubts and scruples about the use of the term *Sabbath* under the gospel—you cannot rid yourselves of a deep sense of the importance of a day of rest to the world

at large.   Hence the resolutions of your churches
and conventional bodies, with regard to the profanation of what you call the Lord's day.   Hence
your plain, out-spoken censures of running cars,
stages, steamboats, and other public conveyances,
on this day.   Hence your griefs and lamentations
over those who make it a day of recreation or
mirth.   Hence your readiness to co-operate with
those bodies which are organized to suppress, if
possible, the violation of what is called the Sabbath.   We admire the principle which governs you
in all this ; but we regret that it is not *regulated*
by a better understanding of the subject.

  If you would promote right principles, you
must be careful that your proofs, and examples
for illustration, are pertinent, and free from all
uncertainty.   We are fully persuaded, that your
Recommendations and *Pledges*, your *Resolutions*
and *Associational Acts*, will always meet with de-
feat, until you can fortify them by a law of God,
so clearly expressed, that it will urge and goad
the violater's conscience wherever he may go.
The consciences of guilty men cannot be reached
by the method you are pursuing.   You behold
them desecrating the Sunday, and, in order to
make them lay it to heart as a sin, you bring
down upon them—what?   Apostolic example?
New Testament intimations, and far-fetched inferences ?   No.   None of these do you think of em-
ploying.   But the *Law*, the all-searching, sin-re-
buking *Law* of God, is the only means you think
of in such a case.   Nothing else suits your pur-
pose, be your *theory* what it may.   But hear their
reply.   " Is the law of the commandment upon

us TO-DAY? That it was YESTERDAY, we allow; for it says, " *The seventh day.*" That the law of the commandment lies against us *every* day, you will not pretend; but only *one* day in seven. If that one day was *yesterday*, you are yourselves as guilty as we; and we, therefore, feel comparatively comfortable. To be sure, some sense of the necessity of keeping the Sabbath holy, does at times rest upon our minds; and our consciences, for the moment, reproach us; but when we see you, and all the Christian world, living in the neglect of it, we feel quite easy again, and think our sin to be but a light one." Such may not be their precise language, but it is the exact expression of their hearts' feelings. Thus even the law fails in your hands, because you attempt to make it speak *what it will not speak.*

If you ask *us*, " Do *you* meet with success in attempting to reach the conscience of guilty, unbelieving men?" we reply, that we have no difficulty, except so far as you, and the whole body of observers of the first day, stand in the way. We bring them to admit, openly and honestly, the claims of God's law, and a sense of guilt momentarily rests upon them. But immediately they turn to contemplate *your* practice, and their hearts become hardened. We do, therefore, affectionately, but earnestly, invite you to consider, how tremendous is your influence toward perpetuating Sabbath profanation in the land. Your numbers, your learning, your talents, your wealth, your general respectability, all combine to operate with overwhelming effect in this matter.

Our observations, if correct, go to show what a

source of danger the Sunday heresy is to the Moral Law. The Sabbath is a most important precept of this law, " the golden *clasp*," as an old writer quaintly observes, " which joins the two tables together; the *sinew* in the body of laws, which were written with God's own finger ; the intermediate precept, which participates of the sanctity of both tables, and the due observance of which, is the fulfilling of the whole law." This important precept is either set aside entirely, or its edge and keenness so muffled by a transfer to another day, that the united efforts of the church can do little or nothing toward impressing it on the conscience. Here, then, is a relaxation of the standard of morality ; and while the standard is relaxed with regard to this one precept, in vain do we look for the Law, as a whole, to appear glorious in the eyes of men.

This remark will be strengthened, if we consider to what inconsistencies the advocates of Sunday are driven. Some, in their zeal to defend it, even go so far as to deny the Moral Law to be a rule of conduct to Christians. Others, though they admit the Law to be a rule of conduct, cannot relieve themselves of at least *seeming* to undervalue it. When the Sabbath discussion is out of sight, they speak out clearly, and without equivocation, giving the fullest proof that they regard the Law as the unchangeable standard of obedience.

But at other times they reason from the New Dispensation in a manner so vague and indefinite that one is puzzled to tell whether they regard the Gospel as enforcing strict obedience to the Law or not. Now he that is established in the clear truth, is hampered with no such difficulties. There is with him not only the naked and abstract admission, that the Moral Law is unchangeably binding, but there appears such a beautiful and perfect conformity between this admission and the principles he inculcates, that the most common minds are struck with it, and every doubt is scattered.

While you are fettered by such difficuties, is there no danger that the Law will lose its sacredness in the eyes of the people? Surely there is. There is danger, also, that your system of theology will be corrupted in other particulars. Error goes not alone. Could an opinion exist in the mind, circumscribed and isolated, without affecting any of our other principles, it would be comparatively harmless. But it is not more a truth, that a man who utters one falsehood is obliged to tell twenty more to hide it, than that he who supports one error is obliged to forge numberless others to give consistency to his creed. It is also a truth, which reflection and daily observation will confirm, that nearly if not quite all the heresies which ever infested the church of God, are traceable to some loose notions concerning the moral law. Nothing, therefore, can be more necessary, than that our creed give the greatest possible prominence to the law as a standard of holiness; and that our customs be in perfect conformity with our creed.

Brethren, can we hope that the subject on which we have addressed you will receive your prayerful attention? Almost your entire denomination has slumbered over it; but may we not hope that

you will now awake ? May we not hope that it
will be discussed in your private circles, and in
your public assemblies ; in your Bible classes, and
in your Sunday schools ; that it will be studied by
your ministers, and by the people in general ; and
that every one will, in the deep desire of his soul,
pray, " Lord, open thou mine eyes, that I may
discern wondrous things out of thy law."

But if, on the other hand, we see a disposition
to pass it by with cold neglect—an unwillingness
to look the question in the face—an attempt, on
the part of your teachers and leaders, to hush it
up as a matter of no importance—a studied effort
to lead the people away from it, when they are
disposed to examine—or teaching them that it is
the spirit, rather than the letter of the law that
God requires—we shall be constrained to apply
the language of Him who spake as never man spake
—" EVERY ONE THAT DOETH EVIL HATETH THE
LIGHT, NEITHER COMETH TO THE LIGHT, LEST HIS
DEEDS SHOULD BE REPROVED." John iii, 20.

www.ingramcontent.com/pod-product-compliance
Lightning Source LLC
Chambersburg PA
CBHW032140080426

42733CB00008B/1142